Footprints of A Wandering Mind

By Maribel Linares

FIRST EDITION

First Printing, 2009

ISBN 978-0-615-24208-8

Printed in the United States of America

Dedication

This book is dedicated to all who see the cup half full, and drink life up. To all who accompanied me on this journey and allowed me to walk a part of it alone when I needed to.
To all who love and hope and believe:

You inspire me with your grace each and every day.

I thank you all.

Table of Contents

Footprints of A Wandering Mind

By Maribel Linares

"Tears are the heart's way of melting with emotion."

Abeni

Crumpled on a dirt floor, clutching a rag doll,
Abeni sobs so silently she seems almost asleep
The tears trickle into ashen earth
The girl they prayed for is hurt.
But no one is there to console her,
No warm arms to stem the tears and hold her.
This is just the marriage prize,
A passage into getting older.
The razor blade has taken away flesh
And imprinted the aching child forever,
With the brand of self-hatred.
Like a scythe that cuts down the graceful strands
Of wheat that sway in the gentle breeze,
All of her innocent dreams are seized.
Abeni, the girl they prayed for, is only eleven.
Her mother tells her to hush her mouth,
That now she will make a good and honest wife.
She has forgotten her own pain, no doubt,
So bad she'd threatened to take her own life.
But now she frowns and looks away,
What's done is done, no use in crying.
She reaches for Abeni's doll and snatches it
As if to say, "You won't be needing this".
She's cruel and unrelenting, but Abeni hands it over.
She understands, somewhere inside the shattering pain
That obliterates all loving ties of mother to child.
That used to be her mother's doll, before she became a bride.

"Memory paints life according to its whim, in the darkest inks or the brightest hues, its fickle fancy dictating all history with a mythical bias."

Alexandria

House of treasures, Golden domes reaching to arid azure skies.

Sun beams cascade down to jewel-encrusted

Balustrades like skeins of translucent silk.

Walls engraved with hieroglyphs and prayers

To Most Sacred Allah enclose jasmine gardens.

Monkeys climb these orchard walls,

Capering in joyful freedom.

Did Buddha sit under such a pomegranate tree?

Did Confucius read the books upon his knee?

Did Zoroaster come in fraternity to preach,

Clutching in his blessed hand, a peach?

The Black Sea and The Red have secrets,

And men have witnessed glory on their banks,

But who can dream of such as is the Nile ,

Where lords of wisdom flooded their ranks?

Europe hath not such a pearl,

As Egypt brought to birth.

No man can know how much it hides,

Nor how much it is worth.

"Patience, patience is the thing. When you slow down, life catches you by surprise, taps you on the shoulder and says, "Hello", with a smile."

An Ode to Heroes

You stare off into space, your face that of a child whose hero of
epic proportions has just fallen short at the worst possible time.
You mourn the death of popular myth because it forces you to
be accountable for your own world.
The burden of creation is foisted upon you.
Another day, another dollar, you state,
As you hurry to your place of work.
Daydreams a brief respite from the reality you hate
The calls you avoid, the duties shirked.
But real reality is only as real as you make it.
Realistically speaking, we are all heroes in our own right.
We are born imperfect and yet somehow find the tools to fight.
You envy the stars on TV, forgetting that not long ago,
You were one.
A whisper from the mouth of Consciousness,
Uttering Universal Law and philosophy.
You are your own hero, but admitting that would mean
Accepting that no one else is climbing up your fire escape.
The things you put off yesterday will still be here today,
And when friends choose to walk away,
No magic wand can make them stay.
You are your mother, giving birth to yourself.
You are your father, teaching yourself the tough lessons of
survival.
You are your sister, growing up while holding on to fond
memories Of a childhood where only your opinion of yourself
mattered.
You are your children, full of the knowledge that you are fully
Capable of creating all of your tomorrows today.
All of this and yet you still look over your shoulder, into the
Shadows, still trying to lean on someone else for answers.
But the truth is, it is your own shadow you must create,
Tall in the face of the rising sun.
A long walk to glory, but fear not. You've just begun.

"Giving your all and failing is better than giving up."

An Attempt To Traverse A Galaxy

If you fail, all the world may collapse beneath your feet.

You will crush the yielding earth

And doom its vibrant song to eternal quiet.

Your ears will burst, so strong will be the deafening silence.

A black hole, an empty crust.

A burning core.

To be forever empty of life and sound,

Forever full of galaxies of guilt.

If you fail, it will be a shame.

But if you never try, it is travesty.

"Joy is not so much the absence of sorrow, as the capacity of the child-like heart to always employ the means to entertain itself, no matter what the weather."

Blackout

Mercury sizzles in the cylindrical tube.

The walls sweat, beads of perspiration

Make your hands slippery

As you steady yourself so as not to faint.

In the darkness, your apartment pants for air

Like a naked man trapped in a box.

There is nothing to drink to cool your thirst.

Nothing that has not thawed out,

Or melted to a lukewarm mess.

The refrigerator stares back at you

Dejectedly, as the kitchen, the last room

In your house, falls victim to the scourge.

Piercing shrieks of shocked children pierce

The night, as they too are left without light.

"We are the mirror of our mate, he or she is the one we run toward, or seek to escape in shame. All we hate or despise in ourselves is reflected in the person we love, and so we must love the darkness within ourselves, if we are to love the light within them. Greater than gold is the alchemy of true love."

Burning Embers

Amidst the burning embers of my mind,
I see the imprint of your face,
Staring out at me from the flames...
The shadows in your eyes are so accusatory,
And I know the trust you had in me is gone.
What I would not do to seal the pages of this book shut,
To open up a new volume and start with you again,
Both of us holding up a pen, side by side together...
We'd write the history of the world according to us.
I know that it's the only way, or else, all's but a pile of ashes.
And your face is just the beginning of a longer goodbye.
Aflame, my thoughts have been my undoing,
Burning a path through our memories together,
Eliminating all proof of your love for me,
Leaving me cold and alone.
But this is a fire that doesn't burn,
It merely obscures my reality.
It blinds me to the truth that's always been there,
Waiting to be seen.
You love me.
You always have.
But you cannot keep me, if you cannot hold me.
Cannot hold me if I make myself my own enemy,
And fail to love myself.
But if you promise to hold my hand, dear one,
Perhaps with enough strength,
I can walk through the fire.
I will see myself in your eyes,
See all the beauty you see in me.
And in your eyes, reflected, I will see my smile.

"Embrace your flaws. They are the nuances of flavor and spice that make your dish unique."

Caliente

You were always so pompous.

What you took for ethereal beauty I characterized as

Anorexia nervosa

I refused to be your "mujer hermosa" and jiggle my curvy butt

On your lap like a contented dog or cat.

Take it as you will, this game is over now.

I would rather that the world call me a sow

Than that you told me I was beautiful.

I much prefer the taste of dulce de leche

To the slapping of our tongues in wet kisses

That are much too bitter and deceitful to show any real love.

I refuse to compromise the languid rhythm of my thighs.

If you don't like me, then why do you stare?

You know it's the spicy heat of me you never could bear.

Tsssssssssssss....I sizzle at 140, 5'7,

Brown eyes and curly brown hair.

"A friend who lifts us up out of sorrow is to be cherished, but a friend who allows us to experience the range and depth of our myriad emotions with unconditional love is a true treasure."

Celebration

I celebrate your wisdom,

Although I never take your advice.

I celebrate your kindness,

When the road begins to wind through

Deserts, and somehow you rescue me.

Forgive me for my ingratitude,

You see it was not my intention.

I would not trade this for a kingdom,

This blissful ignorance has no price.

You would not be you if you did not

Challenge all my senses, and without

My laziness, who then would I be?

There are so many things about you

That merit celebration, so many that

I forgot to mention.

"Imagination is the seed of invention, newly watered with enthusiasm, and waiting for the light of grace to shine upon it."

Celestial

Clouds cuddle together like children hiding

Under white woolen blankets.

Their cerulean cradle rocks them all day

Like their mother in her soft dress.

Every morning it is a different color

As she comes closer to their bed.

Her hair rests on her breasts, burnished gold.

Her cheeks are warm and rosy

With the promise of light and cheer.

Mother Sky bends gracefully in the night

To clutch her husband's arms and pull him

Up from his nap on the purple cot.

Cranky as usual, but unresisting, he rises.

His silvery hair flows down his back like water,

And his pale face is grizzled and gray with age.

Mother Sky knows better.

The couple greets each other with a kiss,

Then separate behind revolving doors.

Tonight, time is ever flowing and complete.

"You ask me who I am, with no interest in where I've come from or who I was before. How then, can you truly know me? I am part and particle of all who've come before me."

Child of Sky, Child of Sun

Mestizo.Ladino.Moreno.Campezino.

From the ruins of Tikal to the jungles

Of the Amazon. I am he-she, child of Sun.

From the misty mountains where coffee grows

To the island regime a slave overthrows.

I am he-she, child of Wind and Rain.

My skin is copper, ivory, golden, black.

I have sung to Gods and harvested corn,

And I have lived through Darkness.

I have woven cloth and bought it for

Three times its worth, all for you.

I have worked for empty coins,

Been spit upon by Spaniards. All for you.

Do not allow anyone to give you any name

But that which you earn for yourself.

I am Child of the Sun and Moon.

They've tried to kill my spirit but I fly

Like the eagle above the ruins they made.

I am Child of Sky, and still I reign.

"Rise with optimism for this new day, for the sun sets on indecision and the darkness of inaction will mock you with every wasted breath."

Cripple

The pieces fit like a child's puzzle,

Forced into place, yet not quite there.

Your spine curves in like a fetus sleeping

Soundly in anonymous pink bliss.

The starched sheets brush against bare toes,

And the ceiling fan brushes you insistently

With feathery touches. A kiss.

The window is closed, shades down.

The sun may as well be the moon.

An entirely different day passes,

Much the same here, in this room.

Inhaling what's exhaled.

"Anger and fear are not evil in themselves. It is when we hold on to them that they take control of us. Let go, and you free yourselves of much sorrow."

The Dilemma of Doing No Wrong

I've seen you waiting at the bus stop,
Staring out at nothing in particular.
The sun plays tag on the rim of your baseball hat
But you wince it all away.
I've seen you standing on street corners
While your friends roll dice and blunts,
Trying not to notice the school children
Who recognize your face. I've seen you at the basketball court,
Watching your bro bully a child much younger,
Hoping no one will notice the hunger, the desire to just fit in.
There are so many of you, everywhere.
The sins you've been acquitted from,
You've already committed, son.
It all boils down to what you should have done.
In the battle between good and evil, evil's all but won.
Sins of omission may still send a boy to prison
For not having the balls to walk in the opposite direction.
Fear of not fitting in should not be your prime concern
Rather, focus on the lessons that are easiest to learn.
Those who cannot walk alone have a troubled path ahead,
Those few who forge their own terrain are happier instead.
It takes so much more time and energy to acquire popularity,
But being yourself is effortless and comes quite naturally.
You may not be first picked in gym, but it's not the end of the
world.
You just may see the light one day, if you're brave enough to
try, to launch yourself with wings unfurled, and fly into the
sky.
You'll soar up there without a care, no drug can beat that high.
To know you can be who you are and not apologize.
I hope you see the truth's out there, the rest is only lies.

"Love is much more than saying, "I'm sorry". It is about accepting apologies."

Empty Nest

There is an odd sound in this house.

The sun sets and shadows settle into crevices,

Dark spots that absorb mirth as well as sorrow.

If you listen closely, it is there.

There is a strange smell as well, that permeates

The rooms, the walls and all that stretches between.

When we inhale we do not breathe, this scented air.

The food we eat is flavorless, our recipes lack flair.

We sit in chairs and lie on beds, but do not rest.

There is something amiss here, to this we must attest.

Have you noticed any of this? I cannot ascertain.

I seem to ignore the obvious now, and still remain.

The arguments are more subdued, bare utterances now.

Masters of the stage, you each played a part

In the disintegration of my youthful heart.

The distant, cold father. The loyal, martyred mother.

It is a wonder you still recognize each other.

Once you were in love, and the future was a garden.

Now you seek to reap fruit, but your seeds won't grow.

Is it any wonder, when the house died long ago?

"In the beginning, children simply *were*. They experienced the world around them with every ounce of their essential being. Now people look in order to see, and think they must become in order to Be. Worst of all, they have no tears, and cannot begin to mourn for all that they have lost."

Faeries and Firelight

Unicorns graze among silver-winged

Faerie Queens,

Bees congregate in flower palaces,

Petal doors bursting at the seams.

A sparkling force-field of faerie dust

Shields supernatural schemes from all

But silly mortals' dreams

Sleep, Sleep, sweet child.

If I could hang from your waist a chain,

It would be of moonbeams.

With it we could travel through the night.

Would laugh to hear the fairies' song,

How like music does it seem.

Joy will fall upon your face like rain,

Love is all we need.

Dance with me upon the heath in the firelight

For nothing can go wrong.

Not when your heart is full of innocence.

Sleep, Sleep, sweet child.

The world of Faerie welcomes thee.

"Otherness is the exotic before it becomes burdened by all who seek to imitate it, and rob it of its novelty."

The Fetishes of the Low-born Tribes

The smoky odor of singed hair hovers above my nose,
And I stare above in horror.

Swathed in the mummifying black robe of an acolyte,
Entering this ritual ignorantly, I wince as my curly tresses
 Are transformed.

They are smoothed to a perfect flatness
With the back of a comb sticky with relaxer.

My torturer's arms flex as she presses against
My neck with the back of her hand.

The tug of war commences, and I, the slave,
Must bend to the will of my master's rope.

Heave, ho! Heave, ho!
She pulls and prods me in my swivel chair.

My eyes fill with tears and the stench of stinging,
Processed hair smothers the scent of the soft perfume
I wear.

I am hoping for a little something new,
But I'd like to be reborn in some gentle, painless way.
Before I regret it all tomorrow.

"Life beckons to us like a child swimming in a lake in summer. Do not stand there on the banks, wondering what it feels like to live in the moment. Jump in! There is always time for worry, later."

The Fire Escape

A little blue lawn chair on the fire escape.

Jars of clumsily molded clay, painted with

All the zest of a Wednesday afternoon.

Plants sit like cats, lazily sucking up sun

Through green, sappy stem straws.

Freckles dot your skin like tiny stars,

And the sky I see in your eyes would

Thaw a thousand winters.

Just like this, as the cars and trucks pass

Like bungling apes in this concrete jungle.

A place for us to breathe when the air below

Is too thick to fill our lungs.

A breath of fresh air today, that's all you

Really came up here for.

Until you kissed me, and rubbed my knee,

And now the fire escape has become our home.

Soon it will rain, you said, and folded me

In your arms to await the first few drops.

"Ignorance is not bliss. Innocence is."

Food for Thought

Shhh, baby…

Hunger is the best sauce.

But Mommy, what will I eat it with?

Imagine a double-decker sandwich,

A glass of cold chocolate milk.

Can I pour as much as I want, Mommy?

Sure, baby…

I promise not to spill any, Mommy.

I know it's just a big dream, but...

No, baby. These glasses never fill up all the way.

Keep on pouring. I'll watch the glass.

You'll see what I mean in time.

"Hope can only be appreciated in the depths of despair. It is a ladder out of a labyrinth, a torch in a cavern. We cannot see it unless we are surrounded in darkness. We cannot experience it until we give up all else."

Golden Age

The world is rife with complication.

Its spirit bleeds on concrete, countryside.

Churches and synagogues suffer desecration.

Child soldiers dodge gunfire, trying to hide.

Epidemic swallows hoards of humanity,

Pestilence sweeps its green scythe abroad.

Young girls starve themselves for vanity,

The rich bear hearts waiting to be thawed.

Where is the reason to justify these pains?

The Earth raises up her arms in supplication

When of her flocks of creatures only dust remains.

Brother killing brother, only to conclude

That the crimson flow is the very same

Under swirling colors of raw flesh.

Generated under the same toil,

Brows anointed with the same sinful oil.

So the mind proves its own enemy, steeling

Itself against even a tiny shard of light.

A streak of hope against a pallid sky.

"To love is to see the wrinkled cheek, and caress it as if it were still smooth."

Grandma

Bending down in her rocking chair out of sheer habit,

Gnarled fingers always curled.

Pieces of old cambric cloth, soft scraps of yarn

Hang like tendrils from her hands.

She works away like a wise old squirrel,

Knows she will no longer be in this world.

A patterned quilt for her grandson perhaps,

This last loving token he will carry in his tiny hands.

Then she may cease complying with worldly demands.

Wrinkled where life's fingers touched her cheeks

With worry, loss and memories,

Her face retains an unnatural glow.

Somehow the rhythm stops in the middle

And her gentle movements slow.

Her eyes stare off to a distant land...

Half a quilt wraps around her lap like a blanket,

Although she will never be cold again.

"It doesn't hurt to laugh, unless the joke's on you."

In the Event of an Emergency

Turn off all lights,

Shut off the faucets

And keep children away from erratic adults.

Keep away from all sharp objects,

And no matter what you do,

Think of pretty things that make you smile.

Do this for three minutes, at least.

After you explain your strange behavior

To your family, destroy this message.

It will self-destruct in 5...4...3...2...

"Indifference makes excuses. Love makes all things possible."

In Time

In time you will see that you misjudged me,
But I will not wait for vindication.
It is an empty justice if it does not serve the both of us.
Mired in guilt, but with clenched fists, I stand renewed
I can live my life without you,
But I cannot live without my dignity.
I will hold my head up high,
Vanquish all my demons,
And be amazed that I ever doubted myself,
Or my power.
My grace.
My beauty.
My wisdom.
And if I am not winded from my victory lap,
I just may have time for a quiet stroll with you.
But only if I have time.

"Happiness is an endeavor requiring our full cooperation in order to be achieved. There is no half-happy, only the acceptance of the meager substitute we allow ourselves to have."

Jack

Climbing up to the giant's world

Of feather-light clouds and golden eggs.

Beans no longer jingle in his ragged pocket

But he whistles as he hauls himself up.

Like one of Columbus' sailors spying land from afar,

He heralds his find aloud.

"I've found the enchanted palace!"

The giant will kill him if he finds him there,

Cavorting with his seven-foot wife

And playing his golden twelve-string harp.

But the dream fades away....

And then he awakens, keyboard flashing

Brightly on his desk.

Papers obscuring his vision and blocking all hope

Of exit from his office.

Another lonely drudge typing away the hours

Before attempting another climb to the glass ceiling.

"When we speak our truth loudly, we sing the song of our birthright to the heavens, and illuminate all humanity."

Just a Taste

These denim jeans will never be tight enough

For you to see my real shape.

It coalesces in reds and greens beyond the

Scope of your perception.

My brainwaves undulate like ocean waves,

Causing you in your manly ignorance to gape.

Only a little taste.

My hair will always be too curly to be the

Silky waves you imagine touching at night.

But whether I comb this mane or let it free,

To prophesize the dawn of my philosophy...

You'll only get a taste of the real me.

I may not be able to carry a tune,

But I sing in my head.

And these enticing beats

That I create will have you dancing soon.

Just a taste is all you'll get,

So get ready to lick your spoon.

"Security is the consolation prize we reach for when we surrender to fear and our dreams fall short of fruition, but is it ever worth the price of our dignity, or our liberty?"

Lucy

She massages one of her bunions with a sore hand.

Scrubbed the walls, mopped the floors,

Did the groceries and cooked dinner.

Sewed a loose button on his shirt because

It was one of the few he really liked.

Here's the mail with a few bills for him.

The rent money was going to come out of his ass,

But it would get there next month, He said.

She made sure the rice wasn't burned today

Because none of the kids were home yet—

Why cook at all if you're just going to burn it? He said.

Although in general her back only hurt

After bending over the bathtub to scour it,

She rubbed it silently as she watched another glass

Slip from her wet hand.

She'd pick it up in time to hear him ask her

What she'd done all day.

"A life without Passion is like an anchored ship in a sea of calm waters, waiting for the raging Storm that will finally move it."

Mâchar'aien

Make me calm, make me better.
Soothe the seething sea that tosses inside my heart
No matter what the weather.

You steer me and lead me to sandy beaches
And ask only that I sit with you.

Make me calm, make me better.
Make me sing while the tide rises, rises.

Make me light, make me better.
My heart is heavy, full of a world of tears.

You breathe across my cheek in cool whispers.
I am the salted rock that erodes with time,
But you ask only that I remember you.

Make me light, make me better.
Make my heart as light as a feather.

Make me feel that eternal flame that was lit so long ago,
Once when we were young.

When we were young with eyes of angels,
And loved like children.

"There is nothing wrong with a little mystery, so long as there is something to hide."

The Mask

Ebbing and flowing with every last breath,

It chases the skies and pierces their depth.

At night it reclines on an ottoman there,

Tucked in between my bed and my chair.

You wouldn't believe all the trouble it took

To look up this sickness inside of a book.

This longing to pull all my sadness inside,

To bury the seeds this barren earth hides.

Just because faces are so explicative,

Doesn't mean mine should seem so indicative.

To me it seems the world is but a lonely hill

That folds within itself however it will.

The wind's pressure bends the leaves of grass

To its pleasure, until they are hollow mass.

Their softness stolen by necessity,

Now a hard bed in which to write my poetry.

I will be sick, like a stunted tree,

Until my true self you may one day see.

"Dreams are the lies we tell ourselves to keep the day's truths at bay. Nightmares are what take over when we finally open our eyes."

Momma

Momma rides on a cloud of smoke, her smile stretching wide
like an accordion. Her son clasps a crayon in his pudgy fingers
and his hand swoops down to his Spiderman coloring book like
an airplane. He is blissfully engaged in minutiae.

When it is time for bed she is just coming back, and they never
meet at the same time, always breaking off at intersections
between high and low, fast and slow.

So when he asks if he can stay up late, she nods, and tilts her
head at him. "Get me a beer."

His little feet shuffle towards the fridge, hoping this time
He won't have to see her face darken like a storm cloud when he
Tells her Momma-deres-nomo-beer-no-food-nowhere-i'm-sorry.

He doesn't want to stay at Auntie's till there's food again;
Her man friend likes to play games when the lights go out.
When he comes back home Momma has new bruises over all
The old ones and there's a sweaty smell all over the house.

So he closes his eyes and clicks his heels like Dorothy, and goes
To a place where there is always food, and no one's hands
Touching him unless it's a hug and kiss goodnight like the kids
Get on TV when they're tucked into warm beds instead of sofas.

Warm beds that cuddle them and hold them until they wake up
Exactly where they were when they feel asleep.

Safe. Sound. Peaceful.

He can smell soap, flowers, and food cooking. And Momma is
awake. She smiles with all her bright white teeth again and
asks him what he wants for breakfast for a change.

"If you seek to know the reason for death, you must ask the right questions. It is not the *what* but the *when* that you fear, and not having that which you now take for granted."

Nacirema

A merry maid laughs softly while at play
Standing in the street.
She does not see the car coming her way,
Her heart skips a beat.
This will be one of her last
She is taken away so fast.
Sirens blare and children scream,
This must all be some cruel dream.

But she is laid on a hospital gurney
Blood pours out of her like a mother's love,
Staining red the minutes as they tick by.

And the driver's gone, he's disappeared
He knows he'll be found not far from here.
Under arrest, he will attest, he knew what he was doing.
That alcohol was his downfall, the reason for his ruin.

It will not matter because down in ICU,
The flat line beeps and the dream is true
Her mother rushes to witness her child's last breath

But when she reaches her bed there's nothing left
But tears, and the sound of the bed linen rustling as
A mother's shoulders rise and fall, rise and fall....
Remembering a merry maid, laughing softly at play.

"Merry is he who takes the narrow path alone, for there is no one left to slow him down."

The Path to Justice

When it is dark, may you have Light.
The road you travel is cloaked with fear,
And all manner of evils exist in the night.

Keep your wits about you and sword near.
A candle shines brighter in the dark than in Light.
Be not afraid to perish for your cause.

There will be others fed by your blood,
And they will follow you.
But if you never go, one less will light the way,
Clear the wild path.

Remember that a candle shines brighter in the dark.
Keep a steady pace, and don't look back.
This is why your eyes face the front of your head.
Glory will not find you sleeping in bed.
Unless you are crowned with the roses of the dead.
Do not let the Light die.

"Beauty is not reflected in dull glass, but in the eyes and hearts of those who love us best."

Periwinkle

If there was less of her perhaps

She'd get more in the world.

Chiffon dresses instead of cotton denim,

Crisscross ankle-tied sandals, no sneakers.

If her face lost some of its roundness,

Perhaps then, people would see her eyes...

They were always such a periwinkle hue,

A gentle breeze of purple mixed with blue.

If there was less of her to see,

Then perhaps his desire to would be greater.

Rather than imagining she was another girl.

She was always such a good listener.

She never judged, always took his side...

Ironically enough, she wished there was less

Of her, so he could see there was so much more

To her than met the eye.

If only she could shrink her body, then maybe...

He'd see how big her heart was.

"Loneliness is a tragedy of denial, a separation from the Light that shines within us all."

Plain Jane

Plain Jane, with dull brown eyes that stared blankly

At the world, wondering why the sky was

So blue when all she saw was black.

Plain Jane, always wanted to have a baby someday,

That would love her like none of the boys

She loved could ever do.

Plain Jane,

Why were you so difficult to understand?

Was it just the world in your head that was so far,

So far away?

Or have you been gone much longer

Than anyone took time to notice?

Plain Jane, I'm sorry if we never saw you cry.

Plain Jane, I'm sorry you thought you had to die.

"There is nothing quite like the manifestations we embody through the work of our hands. Newly created, these portals into other worlds can be ventured into at will, and represent to us the immortality of the soul."

Pottery

Moist mishmash of manmade manipulation, brown and gray.
A funnel of fuel in your hand, and spinning into clay.
Earth will be born inside, and yield to the churnings of a small spoon.
Dig for seeds of souls, germinated in this vast world's soil.
Carve the runes of preservation in order to commemorate this day.
The ink will dry as it stains the base, settling into etchings.
When it bakes in the oven you will have a piece of me to keep forever.

"Laughter bubbles with a frothy effervescence, like a fresh champagne, to mark life's happiest moments."

The Queen of Sherbet

Cautious not to let even a drop of soft,
Saccharine sherbet stain her sheets
She licks delicately at her bottom lip.
Today, the flavor is peach.

Reclining on a bed of pillows, teddy bears
And rolled up clothes she has taken off
The Queen revels in her nakedness.

The ceiling fan cools her plump body,
And she envisions male slaves fanning her.
Clutching the remote control like a scepter
She changes channels like conquering continents.

A flick of her fickle wrist and she chooses,
Sighing contentedly. Jerry Springer again.
Reaching for her carton, she smiles.

"You say you have a split personality,"
 The topic for the day.
The crowd rips into ribald laughter. Ahhh...Peasants.

"We are here, with our eternal drive to dream, to love, to create and to experience. There is no more meaning, more meaningful than that."

River

She wanted utter and total freedom.

She liked windows because they let her look

Out into a world she would one day own.

Doors, she liked almost as much, because they

Allowed her to pass through portals.

But they also closed.

She liked to wear her hair loose, uncombed

Except for the wind's rude fingers.

It gave her joy to climb mountains and trees,

To fish in rushing rivers and eat wild fruit.

Water washed her, sang to her, led her away

Sometimes she would wade hip-deep in water,

Trying to find the end, the beginning of

Where it led, where it would take her next.

But there was neither a start nor finish.

She liked water best, because like her,

It was constant and incessantly in motion.

"Two hearts are merely the soul of one, reflected."

The Silver Cord

Something like a celluloid dream,
You roll across my computer screen like electric joy.
Setting aside all other irrelevant tasks,

I bask in this momentary planetary shift.
We are able to traverse the oceans and time,
Like molasses in a jar, drips richly slow.

At any other time, this would be lunacy.
Will this end in heartbreak, or worse?
A chilly indifference that cracks our mirror to the
Cosmos?

You are but a figment.
But still I await the appointed hour,
And like a moth to a flame, hover still.

I hope that later on, when we are both older
And wiser in our years, we'll realize it all.
We'll see each other as what and who we are.

But let me sit here for now, communing with you
Until we are both too tired to sleep.
Too feverish to dream of how reality must be.

"Youth is the envy of Old Age, until it destroys itself, and all hope for the latter to exist. These are evil times when ghosts walk the streets and men in wicked wars do persist."

Toy Soldiers

Before the cold words can fall from their lips
Like stunted growths of withered trees,
They bear arms upon their knees.

Before a curtain of dull gray covers eyes and blinds them
To human sufferings.
Before kinship becomes a loosened chain of rusty links,

Pieces of once golden hearts…
Before all is severed, there are boys.
There are streets where life pulses in the cracks,

Where marbles roll endlessly, and the sun dances a jig at
Noon. There are stray cats and ice cream cones, airplanes and
Xylophones…

Until orange and green battle for supremacy.
Then the roofs are no longer made for flying paper
Airplanes, but firing gunshots.

Then the cherub becomes a toy soldier,
His blood as vivid as paint,
As bright as a rose against a barren field of snow.

Here is where the flowers die before they grow.

"Temptation is merely an avowal of an unfulfilled desire, not the denial of a need. If we needed all that we desired, how foolish would we be?"

Tuesday

In the early morn he goes to the bodega across the street,
craving cheese curls.

He sees her blue sunglasses behind the countertop,
And makes a wish:

If you were a cup, I'd hold you all the time.
I could kiss your lips with every sip, but oh, if you were air,
I'd keep you there, and breathe you in.

She does not know of the prophecy unfolding

As he slips his hand in his jeans pocket.

You would look good in leather, she thinks,

As she picks up her latte and drinks.
If you were a little older, I could fix you up with my baby sister.
But you're too young for love, too old for kisses, or
Clasped hands waiting for conversation to break heated silences.
Things being as they are...
You will feed your munchies and play guitar.

"That'll be 80 cents", says the cashier.

He goes and she watches.

"The only thing worse than the door that closes in your face, is the one that never opens."

The Un-sung Love Song

Speaking softly in slow-motion,
The words are pouring from your lips like musical notes.
Your song calls me forth.
La-la-la-la-la....No flute, no pipes.
Just a simple baritone and a smile.
I watch from my camouflaged hiding place,
The wall of flesh that houses my spirit
In a broken silence of sighs.
I am only watching you from afar.
Your song builds stronger weaves,
And as they spin their magic spell, I am enthralled.
By the thread you wrap around my soul when you
open Your mouth,
Unknowingly knowing all of me.
I am only watching you from afar.
You glance up, and see me watching you.
Only a break in the cadence, a small caesura
To the epic poem that is our story.
You just haven't read it yet.

"A mirthless smile, a winter sun that fails to warm, a beautiful tasteless dish. These and more, are to me evoked outside your arms, without your kiss. All of you and yours, I miss."

Waiting to Be Lit

When you finally come, I promise to behave myself.
For the most part.
I know I'm not that easy to understand,
I'll try not to drive you mad.
I'll do my best to keep you happy. If I can.

 If not, then I suppose I failed.
Which would inherently imply I'm staying here
In this maze of Why-Can't-I-Just-Be-Me-
It's-Not-Too-Hard-Is-It?

What is there left to know that cannot be
 Found inside of me?

When you finally come, I promise to behave myself.
I know I'm not that easy to understand.
But I'll try not to drive you mad.
I'll do my best to keep you happy.

The words make sense. At least the words do.

I'm just a candle of good intentions,
Waiting to be lit by you.

"The secret to a good life is taking the time to read the instructions."

Wisdom's Wacky Words

So sometimes sitting sedately stifles...
Generally gloating gets gross gradually.
People pretend potentialities predetermine,
Although all animals arrive at an aim.

Death doesn't delude dedicated dreamers
Into imagining idiotic intangibles.
Maybe making memories means more.

Remembering remarkable roads ridden,
Finally finding friends.
Living life lavishly.
Quoting Quixote quietly.

Taking tidbits to trampy tabbies.
Eating escargots each evening.
Carnally caressing Catherines close.
Kissing K-9's.

Never neglecting necessities
But believing because basically
Truth tells timeless tales.

www.ingramcontent.com/pod-product-compliance
Lightning Source LLC
Chambersburg PA
CBHW020907100426
42737CB00044B/667